A Note to Parents

P9-CCM-725

Read to your child...

★ Reading aloud is one of the best ways to develop your child's love of reading. Older readers still love to hear stories.

★ Laughter is contagious. Read with feeling. Show your child that reading is fun.

★ Take time to answer questions your child may have about the story. Linger over pages that interest your child.

...and your child will read to you.

★ Do not correct every word your child misreads. Say, "Does that make sense? Let's try it again."

★ Praise your child as he progresses. Your encouraging words will build his confidence.

You can help your Level 2 reader.

★ Keep the reading experience interactive. Read part of a sentence, then ask your child to add the missing word.

★ Read the first part of a story, then ask your child, "What's going to happen next?"

★ Give clues to new words. Say, "This word begins with *b* and ends in *ake*, like *rake, take, lake*."

★ Ask your child to retell the story using her own words.

★ Use the five *W*s: WHO is the story about? WHAT happens? WHERE and WHEN does the story take place? WHY does it turn out the way it does?

Most of all, enjoy your reading time together!

"Once you learn to read you will be forever free."
– Frederick Douglass

Copyright © 2005 NASCAR® and
Reader's Digest Children's Publishing, Inc.
Published by Reader's Digest Children's Books
Reader's Digest Road, Pleasantville, NY U.S.A. 10570-7000
and Reader's Digest Children's Publishing Limited,
The Ice House, 124-126 Walcot Street, Bath UK BA1 5BG
Reader's Digest Children's Books is a trademark
and Reader's Digest and All-Star Readers are registered trademarks
of The Reader's Digest Association, Inc.
NASCAR® and the NASCAR® Library Collection are registered trademarks
of the National Association for Stock Car Auto Racing, Inc.
All rights reserved. Manufactured in China.
10 9 8 7 6 5 4 3 2 1

Photo credits: Front cover, page 24 ©2004 Action Sports Photography, Inc.; title page, page 4, 12, 18, 20, 22, 24 (inset of Michael McSwain), 25, 26, 29, 30, 31 ©2004 Sherryl Creekmore/NASCAR; page 6, 9, 10, 14, 16, 21 CIA Stock Photography, Inc.

Library of Congress Cataloging-in-Publication Data

Kelley, K.C.
Racing to the finish : teamwork at 200 MPH! / by K.C. Kelley.
    p. cm — (All-star readers. Level 2)
ISBN 0-7944-0603-3
[1. Stock car drivers—Juvenile literature. 2. Stock car racing—Pictorial works—Juvenile literature. 3. Teamwork (Sports)—Juvenile literature. 4. Teamwork (Sports)—Pictorial works—Juvenile literature.] I. Title. II. All-star readers. Level 2.

GV1029.9.S74K455 2004 796.72—dc22   2004053176

Racing to the Finish

Teamwork at 200 MPH!

by K.C. Kelley

All-Star Readers

Reader's Digest Children's Books™
Pleasantville, New York • Montréal, Québec

It's a great day for a race! Race
fans fill the seats at the huge track.

Flags are waving and people are cheering. Everyone waits for the start of the big race.

On the track, the cars are getting ready for the big race. Each car takes its place on the track.

The cars are bright and colorful. They look like a rainbow lined up on the track.

The driver sits behind the wheel of his mighty car. Soon, he will zoom away at high speed. Right now, he is thinking about the race ahead. As he gets ready, he thinks, *We can do it!*

The driver might be alone in the car. But he is not alone at the track. He has a big crew working with him. NASCAR racing is all about teamwork!

Racing teamwork starts long before race day. First, many people work together to build the car. They use special tools and even computers!

A special crew builds the car's engine. The powerful engines are made of hundreds of parts. Each part helps make the engine go.

Race teams need a lot of gear.
The gear is packed in big trucks.
Truck drivers bring the gear to
the track.

The drivers park the trucks in the middle of the giant track. The trucks carry everything the teams will need to race—and to win!

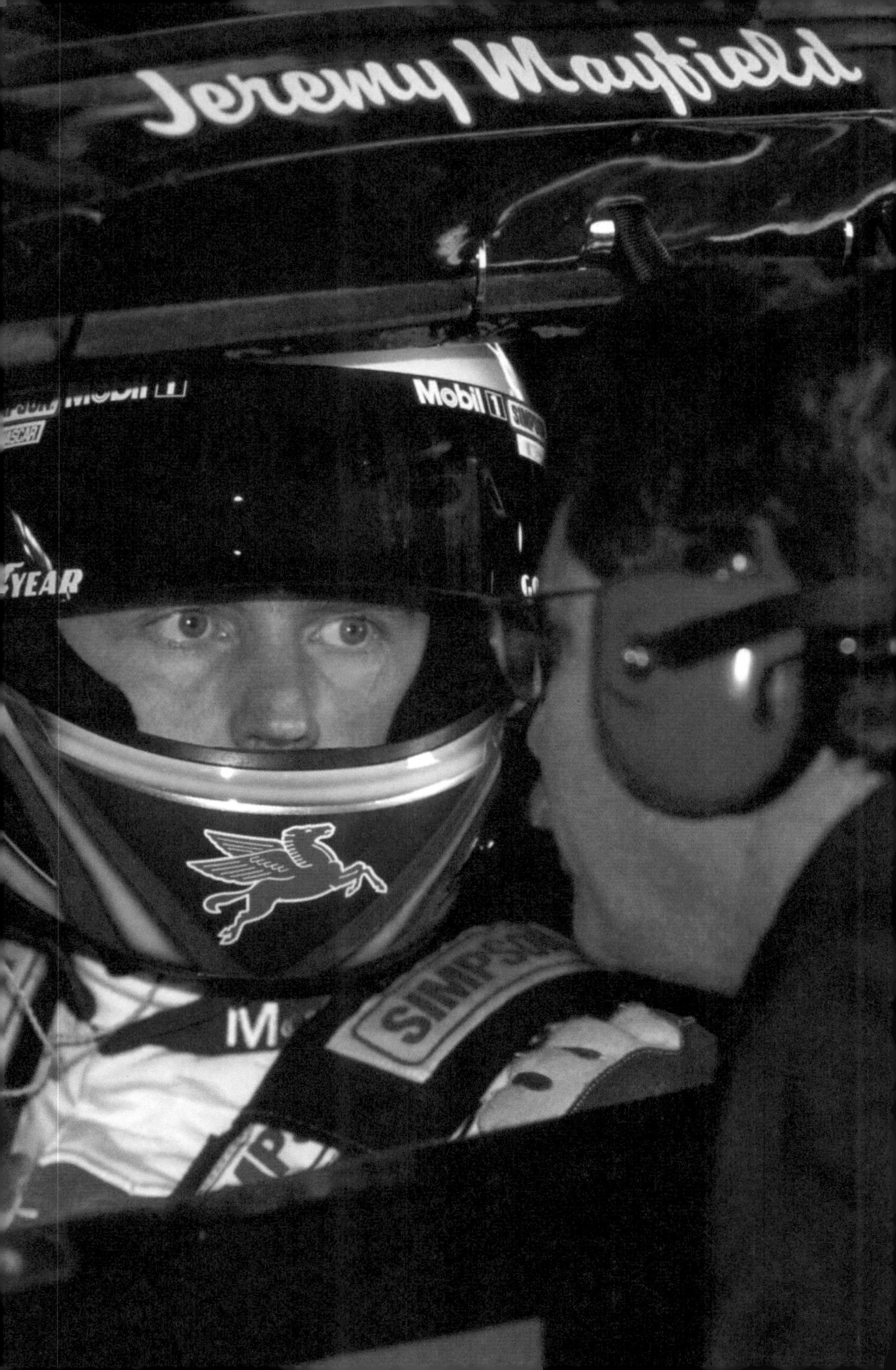
Jeremy Mayfield
Mobil 1
Mobil 1
SIMPSON

Who is the captain of the racing team? It's the crew chief. He is in charge of all the workers on the team. A crew chief makes sure the team is trained and ready for the race.

Before the race, the crew chief meets with the driver. They talk about how to drive in the race. Crew chiefs are very important teammates!

During a race, a driver must stop to get gas and new tires for his car. It's time for more teamwork!

When the driver stops, the pit crew goes into action. They leap over a low wall. Each member of the crew has a job to do. There's not a second to spare!

The first man over the wall carries
a jack. With a mighty push, the
man uses the jack to lift one side of
the car off the ground. Two other
crew members carry huge tires
over the wall.

Two more teammates leap onto the track. They carry special tools for changing tires. They remove the old tires. Then they put new tires on the car. They can do all this in just a few seconds!

Two other crew members carry tall, heavy gas cans. They fill the car with fuel in no time.

When the last tire is put on, the jack man lowers the car. The driver zooms onto the track, ready to race again. The pit crew has done its part. Now other team members take over.

The most important member of the race team is the driver. His team has worked hard for many days to get his car ready. He has worked

with his crew chief to plan the race. The driver's skills have been tested for years. He is ready.

From behind the wheel, the driver talks with the crew chief using a special radio. The driver's radio is built into his helmet. The driver and the chief talk about how to run the race. They decide when to make pit stops. They talk about the other cars on the track.

High above the track, other teammates watch. They are called spotters. They let their race team know what is happening far up the track. Knowing what is ahead helps the driver make the right moves.

The race is nearing the end. The driver looks for a way to pass the other cars. The spotters tell the driver how many cars are ahead of him on the track. The crew chief makes a suggestion. Look for a chance to pass on the next lap!

The cars are speeding around the track. They are just inches apart! Suddenly, the driver sees an opening. With a roar of his engine, he rockets into first place!

The final lap has begun. The driver is ahead of all the other drivers. His teammates are cheering him on. So are the fans.

Finally, the hard work of the whole team pays off! The driver zooms under a checkered flag. He and his team have won the race!

Now comes the best part of teamwork. The hard-working winning team heads for Victory Lane! The fans cheer. The driver lifts the winning trophy. At first, he lifts it alone.

But soon he passes it around. He knows that many people helped him reach that winning moment. In racing, teamwork means trophies!

Words are fun!

Here are some simple activities you can do with a pencil, crayons, and a sheet of paper. You'll find the answers at the bottom of the page.

———— ★ ————

1. This book is all about teamwork. Two words can sometimes "team up" to make a new word. Match up the words on the left with their "teammates" on the right to form a new word.

home	bow
every	track
rain	shine
race	one
sun	work

2. The race cars pictured in this book all have bright, bold numbers painted on their doors and roofs. If you had a NASCAR race car, what number would you pick? Draw a picture of a race car with your number on it.

3. The sentences below all have words that are missing letters. Using the hints, fill in the correct letter or letters to complete the words below.

• The race car __ooms around the track really fast.

• The members of a pit crew leap over a low wa__ __.

• Drivers strap themselves in with a safe__ __ belt.

• Trucks carrying race cars park in the mi__ __le of the racetrack

4. Can you think of the opposite of each these words?

fast	winning
low	loud
ahead	hot

ANSWERS:
• homework; everyone; rainbow; racetrack; sunshine
• zooms; wall; safety; middle
• fast/slow; low/high; ahead/behind; winning/losing; loud/quiet; hot/cold